Copyright © 2018 Selene Gentzler
ISBN 978-1-387-94042-4

All rights reserved. This book or any portion thereof may not be reproduced or used in any manner whatsoever without the express written permission of the publisher except for the use of brief quotations in a book review.

First printing, 2018.

LuluPress.com
Morrisville, NC

www.volleybloggingmom.com

Club Volleyball 101: Basics for Club Volleyball Beginners
By Selene Gentzler

Copyright 2018

Table of Contents

Beginnings and Where to Start	4
Open Gyms	8
Tryouts- A Guide for Your Athlete to Read	16
The Offer	22
In Season Routine	27
Tournaments	32
Season Extras	43
Return on the Investment, Recruiting	49
Conclusion	54
About the Author	55
Appendix	60
Recruit Resources	60
Player Questionnaire	62
Glossary	65

Beginnings and Where to Start

The start of high school season is about to begin.

A seasonal ritual that happens every year. It has new dynamics, new challenges, new dramas, and hopefully great expectations.

Another season ritual is club coaches start to perk up, put their ear to the ground, and start watching players in their area that they would like to play for their organization. In Pennsylvania coaches are only supposed to talk to parents regarding athletes playing for clubs. They could also mention it to the high school coach. Realistically do not be surprised if this rule is viewed as a "if you want to" follow it type of rule. Be sure if your athlete is considering club to let them know that any/all conversations should be directed to you as the parent.

For those who are very new to the sport. Club volleyball is an opportunity for young athletes to participate in volleyball after the traditional high school season. There are a full range of club types with a variety of offerings, club fees, and costs. Each has their own flavor and focus.

More on that later.

If someone had asked me if I would be participating in this world of sports about five years ago I would have told them they were out of their minds. But my children wanted more from their playing experience so we ventured into the world of club volleyball. And what an adventure it has been.

Thus the birth of this book.

So your child loves volleyball. They would like to learn how to play better. Practices at the high school level often focus on preparing for the next game. With a two a week game schedule, three practices maybe two if coaches give Fridays off for football games there really isn't enough time for an athlete to grow in the game. Don't get me wrong, they will improve. The game of volleyball is about repetition, becoming very familiar about the game in game/game-like experiences, and how to work alongside five other players on the court who are working to do the same thing. Practice, more touches on the ball, instruction are all key to an athlete improving.

WHERE TO START:
1) Ask other parents if they participate in club volleyball. Ask about their experience with the club, their daughter's experience, and different aspects they found helpful or challenging.

2) Have your child ask their volleyball friends if they play club volleyball and who do they play for.
3) Do your research before the tryout. To find out about the local clubs in your area you can Google it.
You can also go to the USAV site that lists the regional sites and links http://www.teamusa.org/usa-volleyball/membership/regions
In Pennsylvania area it is the KRVA (Keystone Region) http://www.krva.org/
Go to Juniors tab, Junior Girls clubs http://www.krva.org/juniors_girls_clubs.php
(This is a listing of the USAV sanctioned clubs in PA)
4) Go to the club website if they have one. Contact the director with questions. Clicking the name of contact will open an email with the contact's email to write to them. I would suggest this and copy yourself in the email. Many of these individuals juggle many other aspects of life. The email will allow them to respond to you at a time that is convenient for them and as a reminder to follow up for you.
5) Attend open gyms to get a feel for the club facilities, coaches, and be able to inquire for more information regarding the club.

6) Talk often with your athlete. Help them define their goals with the sport. Help them figure out what they want to gain from the club experience. This could range from spending time with friends, improving for the high school team, or in my case a child who was inspired to be better by watching the Olympics and still has big dreams. Whatever their reason will also be helpful in the club tryout process, decision making, and success in their experience.

7) Define what you are willing and able to invest financially. Money talks with your child will help them understand the why/why not a club may not be an option. The talks may include your expectations for them to contribute to club costs or what they may have to sacrifice as a result of their participation. Life lessons can be learned such as how larger financial decisions and budgets are made. Including them in that part of the process can be beneficial.

Club volleyball is an investment in money and time for not just the athlete but the entire family.

Doing the research and defining the purpose of being involved in club will assist in getting the returns on the investment in the long run.

Here's to great beginning

Open Gyms

Open gym time is an opportunity to get a preview and feel for a club organization. For the seasoned parent this is a time to go find out what is on the agenda for your child's favorite clubs and see who else is considering trying out for this season. For some families it is to scope out the competition and for others what players they might wish to avoid during the club tryout process. Be mindful open gyms are NOT a clinic so coaches/directors will probably not coach your child during these sessions. Open gyms are more like fitting rooms at clothing stores to see if the club is a good fit for you and if your athlete is a good fit for the club.

For new parents it could be just the tip of the iceberg to what can be an overwhelming process when the gauntlet, club tryout week, begins for your child's age group.

Things to know:

IS HE/SHE ALLOWED TO ATTEND?

It is the high school coach preferences as to whether the student athlete can play or not play at club open gyms. Typically coaches who have a preference will announce it during practices. Most coaches will allow athletes to attend in street clothes to see the competition and give parents the opportunity to talk to the coaches of the team.

One of my daughter's peer's coach banned attending even club volleyball meetings or a cleanup day. The choice to go or not go is up to you as a parent but understand if your child plays for a team that has post season potential it could put them at risk for not playing due to injury risks or coach's consequences.

BE PREPARED

Prior to attending an open gym it is wise to talk with your child about their goals for club season, what they are looking for and NOT looking for in the club experience. What types of questions do you have for coaches, directors and other parents? Write them down on a note card, notebook or on your phone if you want to be discreet and/or conveniently organized. Typical questions might include

Coaches:
- What is the practice style?
- Coaching type?
- Will they be coaching solo or will other coaches be available with practices?

-Directors:
- What is the average cost for the age group your child wishes to try out for?
- What are the payment schedules?

- What are the proposed practice times for the age group?
- Will extra sessions be available for skills/positional practices?
- If yes is there an extra cost?
- What type of fundraising opportunities is available?

- Parents
- Did your child play for this club before?
- How did you feel about the experience?
- What did you like best? Worst?
- Typically what amount of travel does the team do?
- What types of tournaments does the club attend?
- What extra fees/costs did you experience throughout the year?
- What coaching/director style does the club have?

I am sure there are many more questions that could be asked. Be sure to ask them!

Your child should also be prepared. What position(s) do they want to try out for? What skills do they want to highlight? What skills do they want to tune-up before tryouts, especially for athletes who play a position different in high school than they want to play in club (college)?

PRE OPEN GYM PEP TALK

It is important to chat before entering the gym. Depending on your child this may need to happen BEFORE they are in the car if they like to jam with headphones prior to doing their volleyball thang or it could on the way actually IN the car. The goal is get your athlete focused, hopefully reduce anxieties, and remind them of some of the "rules" of the road.

First and most important. HAVE FUN! If you as a parent are considering your child entering the world of club volleyball please be sure that it will be an enjoyable experience for them. Remind them often this is a choice in life, not life or death, and doing what you love can be work but should never become a chore.

Remind them that as much as they want to have fun, making an impression is important so they should also wish to do their best. Not just to impress potential coaches, but to also take advantage of being around other motivated athletes to improve skills and volleyball awareness/IQ.

Be assertive. When coaches run 6 on 6 drills your child will want to RUN to the position they want to play or ask another athlete who has been playing a position for several rotations for a turn (this goes for tryouts too). Coaches are not going to police court opportunities and I am pretty convinced the definition of fair, nice, considerate, etc. reads differently in the dictionaries of some people.

Less is more when talking about where they plan to tryout. Athletes are not the only ones scoping out who the competition is. Some coaches will ask your athlete where they are planning to tryout. I have seen this be to the benefit of an athlete the club is considering, but I have also seen this be hurtful to an athlete who could be on the bubble. This year might be the first year in 4 years of club I have felt comfortable to be transparent about where we are going. Remind your child that they are not obligated to answer questions if they do not feel comfortable and vague answers such as " my parents and I haven't worked it all out yet but I plan on trying out here(if that is a true statement). You can ask my mom/dad if you want". In our area coaches are supposed to only talk to parents, so have them be sociable and talk volleyball skills but not volleyball business.

I have also found this policy of less is more to be very helpful in the presence of coaches, other athletes, and families. My policy is that any comments, opinions, rants and rages have to wait until the car doors are shut and the windows are up. If your child needs to talk to you be sure it is private and not discussed with others. Word of mouth can be hurtful to your child especially if distorted information is repeated.

COURT AWARENESS

I confess! As a new parent and as a seasoned club parent, I have eavesdropped a lot of conversations. It is how I learned some of the ins, outs, and backwards things of club volleyball. Seasoned parents are very open about club gossip and experiences when they reunite with last year's families. Coaches are also not as covert about conversations either. Watch what is going on around your child on the court.

- Are coaches talking with your child or moving them to different positions?
- Are coaches talking to athletes and then walking over with the athlete to talk to the parent? That might be a sign of a club that recruits prior to tryouts
- Are coaches directing traffic of who plays on what side/team? If yes, who are the athletes they are playing with regarding skill level?
- Who do you see as your child's closest competition and what are they doing well?
- Honestly where do you see your child fitting in with this club?
- How many girls in your athlete(s) desired position?
- Did your child get moved to a higher age group? Being aware of what is going on around you will help with your athlete putting their best foot forward on tryout day(s) and in the decision making process when tryouts are done and offers are given. And be aware of the prickly parent who

under the pressures of competition may not respond to your polite and political correct questions. It's them, not you trust me.

Watch your child's expressions and if you make eye contact be sure to give positive affirmations like smiles, thumbs up, or whatever secret hand signals your family might use. Is your child enjoying the experience? Are the athletes around them positive and encouraging? Are mistakes weighing so heavy that they are not performing to what you know is their potential? Take note of things they do well on the court because many young athletes will only remember the amount of mistakes made coming off the court and will need to be reminded of what they did well.

POST OPEN GYM SUMMARY

Hopefully your child will get into the car bubbling with excitement about how much they enjoyed the open gym, what they learned, who they met, and on and on. If they are not, ask your athlete to share their thoughts, feelings, and analysis of the open gym. If they tip too far negative, point out some of the skills they might have performed well. I had four children playing co-ed club at one time and only forty-five minutes so each one shared three things they did well and three things they wanted to improve upon. If my child is very moody or distraught I usually talk up the good things I saw them doing well until they join in the conversation. If you are unable to get them to talk, wait till later but probably not longer than two days. Many reasons for this such as brooding too long on negatives that may not be reality, self esteem deflation risks, and a host of other not helpful thoughts that could affect upcoming tryouts. Hash out the negatives, pump up the positives and definitely attend more open gyms of that club or a different club. Nerves and negative self talk can wreak havoc on athletes, so much that I have seen very talented athletes become physically ill during this process... Do not allow them to blow things out of proportion or magnify mistakes. Some of the best advice I have ever heard regarding volleyball, is that it is a game of mistakes and the one who makes the least is the one who wins. And how true that is! They need you to keep them level headed and focused on the main things which is showcasing who they are and encouraged toward where they want to go.

The open gym process is an exciting time for exploration and new beginnings. Communication, observation and preparation will help you and your athlete make the most of the time.

Keep it light and fun, but focused on the direction your child wants to go on the volleyball journey.

Tryouts-
A Guide for The Athlete to Read

Tryout time.

This invokes several thoughts and feelings for all involved in the process.

For most athletes it is an exciting time to see old coaches, tremendous friends, and show the skills gained since last season. For other athletes it brings about trepidation of will they make a team, will they do their best, and just the unease of being watched and evaluated. Parents could have an entire dissertation of emotions, actions/reactions, and thoughts running through their heads ranging from newbie experiences to the seasoned parent experience. Directors, coaches, and administrators have their own types of anticipation and mental/emotional demands during the process.

It is the best of times

It is the worst of times.

For the athlete, here are some basic suggestions of how to maximize the tryout experience.

Things to know:

PACK THE NIGHT BEFORE YOUR STOMACH and YOUR BAG

You might have nerves of steel or have been through this before. But trust me you want to make a checklist of items you want to be sure to have for tryouts and pack your bags the night before.

Why a checklist?

To keep you from tearing apart your bag thinking you might have forgotten something that you didn't.

Packing your bag the night before allows there to be no desperate tearing apart of the closet searching for the AWOL kneepad or ankle brace. It makes sure no shoe is left behind!

What about your stomach?

Depending on how early your day has to start for the tryout process, you may or may not be up for a good breakfast, even though your parents will encourage you to. A solid carbohydrate filled dinner with vegetables and fruits throughout the day before will help you have a full fuel tank of reserves to cover the lack of eating and the amount of energy you will exert. And hydrate, hydrate, hydrate the day before and day of.

KNOW THE GAMEPLAN

Tryout day in our region has many clubs with various tryout times all across the area. Most likely your parents have plotted the course for the day of where and when you will be going to different locations. Take a moment to sit down with your parent(s) to discuss what the route plan is. Double check the club website, invoices, and paperwork to be sure of tryout times, locations and just to be sure you have all forms needed for the tryout. Develop a mental plan of what it is you want each club to know about you as an athlete. If you have attended open gyms or talked with coaches/friends you will know potentially who your competition. Preparing mentally is just as important as your parents knowing where they are going and when. Ask questions of the coaches as to how and when offers/invitations are communicated to the player.

DRESS TO BE NOTICED

Some clubs will have a uniform tryout shirt to wear for tryouts. If the club does not, you have the ability to choose what to wear or what not to wear. What **not** to wear is gear from competitive club. What **not** to wear is cut off shirts (some coaches see this as sloppy). What you can wear is a shirt with your high school name on it, a catchy logo, or something bright. This is not only to catch the attention of coaches but possibly help coaches recall when your name/play comes up in the after conversations.

Long haired lovelies – today is not the day to show off your lovely locks. One of the top complaints of evaluators is that young ladies hairstyles get in the way of being able to see the participant numbers. Tryout shirts will most likely have the numbers in the front and back printed on them. If you have to place a number on your shirt, it will most likely be on the back if you plan to pancake balls up to impress coaches. Having a hairstyle that will keep your hair up and away from your participant number will keep from another player getting the credit for your play later when coaches are talking through team candidates.

EAT A GOOD BREAKFAST

As a parent it must be said. Eating a good breakfast the day of tryouts is important. Even if it is just some toast, fruit and yogurt. Depending on how much time you allow yourself between waking up and eating will depend on what type of breakfast you will want to have. Heavy and greasy is not advised. And limit the milk products that create phlegm and may not digest in time for athletic activities. Give yourself plenty of time to digest. But take time to enjoy French toast, eggs, bagels, fruit, waffles, or your favorite breakfast to get a good start to make for a great day!

HIGH ENERGY

Your high school coach may or may not have been a "hustle" style type of coach. Coaches and evaluators are walking in and out of the tryout process so there may be a multitude of times you get to make a first impression. When moving from one drill to the next, do it quickly and hustle. Walking might indicate to a coach that you are out of physical shape or not very motivated to make a spot on their team. Be sure that coaches know you are the one that is going to work hard throughout the season by working hard in tryouts.

IF YOU CAN TEXT AND CHEW GUM YOU CAN AND SHOULD DO THIS

Playing volleyball is a multi tasking sport. Believe it or not, talking on the court is one of the least utilized skills on the court. Hard to believe if you have ever been in a car or bus with multitudes of teammates. Sharing with a hitter how many blockers or what position to hit, calling for the play if you are a hitter, calling in or out for a backrow player whose eyes are on the ball and not on the line, calling where a hitter's shoulders are pointing or if they plan to tip are some of the ways you can make an impression on the court with coaches. Another impressive communication type is cheering other athletes on when they have a great play and cheering from the sidelines for those playing on the court. Also an important skill to get noticed for recruiting by college coaches. It is important for coaches to be able to see your skills not only as a great player but as a supportive teammate as well.

REMEMBER THE WHO AND WHY

Lastly, and most important…. remember who you play for.

It is not your parents, the future college coach, your current high school coach, your potential club coach…

The who **is you**!

And the why, ask yourself that. Answer it.

What is the why that gets you back on the court when every muscles ache?

What is the why that helps you overcome bad days, team meltdowns, stressful schedules, etc?

When you find your why, write it down on a note card, and carry it with you.

"Somewhere behind the athlete you've become and the hours of practice and the coaches who have pushed you is a little girl who fell in love with the game and never looked back... play for her." Mia Hamm"

The Offer

The offer. Much anticipated moment after a nerve wracking tryout which may feel like an eternity.

Once again this may vary depending on the area in which you live. In some areas the tryout will give you an opportunity to receive an offer to play for the club with no details as to which team, teammates or positions you would be playing for. It is strictly an invitation to play for the club. Other areas of the country the offer is specific with position and team, whether national/regional/travel that the player is being invited to. It is also not an uncommon practice for tryouts to be at the same time which forces athletes to be limited in the clubs they can tryout for which it can be a do or don't situation for club season. Be sure to find seasoned parents in the area to help navigate what to expect.

PRE" WHAT IF" SCENARIO GAME

Once your child has completed tryouts and can assess where they fit in with the competition it is helpful to begin the "what if" discussion. What if you were offered the position you want but it is a regional team or not quite the position you were seeking on a national team? What if you were offered a position on a highly competitive team or a position on a team with your friends? Whatever scenarios that you could see being an impasse or challenge in the decision making process will allow your child begin to process and work with what each scenario might mean to them.

MURPHY EXISTS

Even with all of the facts, projected scenarios, and discussions when the offer arrives more times than not the reaction parents expect is not what the athlete does. If you have ever given a Christmas gift to a young person, you know this reaction. You think they will love it and upon opening it and the gift is received like a skunk in a box. Nose goes up, eyes begin to leak, and unexpected words come out of their mouths. Parents and athletes both need to be prepared for this reaction of when conjecture meets reality. It is a life lesson that all parties will survive.

PATIENCE IS A VIRTUE

If your athlete has tried out for more than one club, be patient for each club's response. For some clubs it can be a complicated process to decide which athletes will fit best into their program. In some regions it is required that communication as to whether an athlete has or has not made a team is required. If the time allotment the club said It would have a response has passed then contact the coach and/or director. Many areas have a time constraint on when you need to respond to the offer so it is important not to wait too long. Be sure all offers are on the table before making a decision as once a choice is made it is binding.

COMPARE APPLES TO APPLES

Hopefully the prep work has been done to evaluate the coaching staff, expected tournament schedule, costs, and other important aspects of each club. Here are some reminders of things to watch for.

- Is coach travel costs included in the tuition fees?
- How many tournaments require one, two, or three night stays? Are they stay and play tournaments which often require a percentage of parents to stay at often high priced hotels?
- What is the background and experience level of the coaching?
- Are there strength and conditioning opportunities? Is it included in the tuition or a separate fee?
- Are there positional practices? Is it included in the tuition or a separate fee?
- How many players are on the team? There is a twofold concern here. A smaller team will mean for more reps in practice and court time. But puts the team at risk for challenges should players become injured, sick or quit. A larger roster will lessen rep opportunities in practice, potentially

less play time, but also often reduces costs. Where does your child rank is important in relation to playing time. It is not uncommon for bigger programs to have players that are considered "practice players" but pay the same fees as athletes who play every tournament.
- Does the tournament schedule meet your child's goals? Local recruitment, tough competition to improve skills, social expectations, etc.

If you are uncertain of the answers to these questions be sure to contact the coach and/or director to be clear where your athlete stands prior to making the decision. Nothing is worse than leaving stones unturned to find the answers later on which might have directly affected the decision.

CRITICAL TIEBREAKER

The one standout aspect in making a decision between offers has consistently been the coaching. The coach's **current** volleyball knowledge about the game and industry is critical especially if your athlete has big dreams and aspirations. Volleyball is much like the technology industry where keeping up with the needs to the market will be more beneficial to your athlete in the long run. A coach that is capable to address a variety of personality types and be willing to address the challenges teams face in the maturing process of the game and individually. Coaches who utilize every minute with a well planned practice agenda will be a better investment versus a wing it approach. Whether a coach has working relationships and respect among college coaches is also important for those athletes wanting to be a part of a successful college program. Quality instruction and guidance will grow the athlete more than any other aspect of the game.

LIFE IS ABOUT CHOICES

After all the analytics and information at the end of the day there is one main thing that must remain true. It is the athlete's choice and life. A young athlete could be presented with an amazing opportunity but if they are not in the right mindset or it is not their choice, it could be worst 6 plus months of life for athlete and parent. The offer decision is just one in many. The greater lesson is in the ownership of the process and owning, navigating, and negotiating the choice that is made.

In Season Routine

Offer accepted. Now the real work and fun begins. Most clubs will have a parent meeting. At the meeting topics will be discussed like club philosophy, tournament schedules, and give players and coaches a chance to get acquainted before the first practice. For parents it is also a time where any contracts between you and the club, payments, and basic information that was not attained during the tryout process will be requested. Some clubs will take pictures for player profiles for recruiting purposes and may even have a practice that day.

PRACTICES

Club practices are not like high school season practices. Most club practices are 2 to 3 times a week for 2-3 hours each depending on age group and level of tournament competition the club chooses. The practices will consist of warm up drills, varied skills drills, positional work, and actual play. Higher level clubs will often require coaches to have a structured timed layout of practice for the team with expectations to adhere to the schedule. Also higher level clubs will cross train players. If your athlete is a setter then they will participate in drills that will be defense focused or if your athlete is a middle then they will participate in drills that involve setting. Volleyball athletes at this stage are a work in progress and the philosophy of developing the entire athlete in all volleyball skills it is beneficial to the possibilities for the future. Practice is where your athlete should receive equitable repetitions/touches on the ball Conversations regarding expectations for attitude and effort during practice should occur and possibly goals the player wants to achieve in practice. Evaluations during practice will be where most coaches will assess how much competition court time a player will see during tournaments. Although your athlete survived tryouts and was offered a position on the team it does not translate to fair and equitable playing time at tournaments. It is important that your athlete makes every ball and practice count.

TO WATCH OR NOT TO WATCH

Some controversy exists about whether parents should watch or not watch practice. First I believe this decision should start between a player and a parent. Each athlete is different in their desire to have their parent attend practice. Some athletes get more nervous and feel more pressure when a parent is watching practice. Practice is where mistakes are allowed and expected to be made so they can be corrected. Depending on the type of child and parent, a parent watching practice could detract focus from working through learning skills needed to improve. Parents who grimace and instruct their athlete during practice, known as helicopter parents, should possibly consider not attending practice. During practice might be a great time to grocery shop, catch up on your favorite shows, or go out with other parents for dinner.

The benefits of watching practice is some children want their parents to be present. Families with multiple children playing sports, it is sometimes the equalizer of being watched if parents are divided when watching actual matches. For a parent it also may help put things in perspective from reality versus teen perception. An observed tendency is for players to keep full record of all the mistakes made during practice and not so much the positive growth achieved. Witnessing first hand will help give a different perspective and be good talking points for the drive home. One of the biggest challenges as a parent is attempting to keep athletes grounded in reality of the situation and not the emotion of the moment. Another benefit of watching practice is being able to talk to parents who will be able to explain more about the game, travel do's and don'ts, and get to know the people you will be on the sidelines with for the next several months. As time moves on parents move from watching every moment of practice to attending practice to get a general feel of the team's progression and spend time with people who become friends along the way.

SEASON EXTRAS – Conditioning -Positional clinics-Lessons

Positional clinics offered by a club should be considered mandatory regardless of club policy. Beyond getting more bang for the buck, practice time is very limited and often dedicated to developing the team as a whole. Positional practices gives specific mechanics and mental mindset for the player's role on the court. Often coaches will be able to take the time to work one on one to address an athlete's challenges. Also it may be a time where varied age groups are on the court at the same time where older athletes can model skills that might not translate the same from a coach's instruction. The value of mentoring is invaluable and if the club you have chosen does not utilize these opportunities, it would be in your athlete's best interest to suggest it.

Strength and conditioning is another extra offered by some clubs. Many volleyball programs from high school to college in all divisions utilize strength and conditioning throughout the year. Depending on the tournament schedule, tournaments can be physically rigorous requiring multiple matches of intense competition for several days in a row. If the club does not have a strength and conditioning resource depending on your athlete's aspirations and schedule, finding a local gym/trainer that can tailor a program for your athlete might be beneficial.

Individual or semi private, where more than one athlete attends, lessons can be another useful option to help your athlete improve volleyball skills. Lessons can give opportunities for the athlete to address the challenges they feel they are having and give another perspective to how to improve their game. One of the other challenges of the sport is the opportunity for repetitions (reps) with the ball. Unlike basketball where athletes can work on skills individually and baseball where batting cages can assist with reps, volleyball requires more than one person and gym space to work on some of the skills for the game. Lessons can also give athletes the extra ears and eyes to help adjust their mental game as well as their physical game.

OUTSIDE PRACTICE

Athletes who excel spend time working on their game away from the court almost as much if not more as on the court. Other ways athletes can improve their game is by running dry drills of their foot work, practicing arm swing in front of a mirror, hand position with setting a ball and mentally review concepts learned in practice that week. It is also suggested by USAV coaches to watch video not only of your own play but high level volleyball to understand the movements of successful players, defense and offense options and the gain a better volleyball IQ for the game. You Tube is a great resource for locating video for college and national team volleyball matches.

Tournaments

Maybe you came across this book to just learn about club and the process. Why would I include information about tournaments? To know what your athlete, and family are getting themselves into. If the cost of the club fees and tuition created a small amount of sticker shock, then be prepared. The costs of club volleyball is just beginning.

The first mega club tournament I attended was the Capitol Hill Classic in Washington D.C. It was amazing, overwhelming and crazy all in the same thought. Let's put this into a numbers perspective. The morning wave typically has 4 teams per court with an average of 10 players per team. With 40 athletes per court and 120 courts, that is 4800 athletes just for the morning wave. Add the afternoon wave and the total is closer to 9600 athletes who most come with coaches, parents, and then there are referees, college coaches and various other folk at these events. It is a far cry from the local high school tournament or event. Now not all tournaments are built the same.

TOURNAMENT TYPES
One day tournaments
- 3-4 pools of teams
- Can be best 2 out 3 , 3rd set to 15 or 2 sets with a summation of win/loss differentials to seed teams

- Can start at 4 to shorten the amount of match time play , may cap points
- Top 1 or 2 teams advance to play offs
- One set single elimination matches for quarterfinals and semifinals
- Final championship best 2 out 3 match
- Typically no or small entry fee
- Hosted by local groups with a better and healthier food selection

The volleyball F.Y.I - Why start at 4? Most referees are trained for match point at 25 not 21, so starting at 4 keeps it uniform and less likely for errors to occur. In these types of tournaments it is common for the top two to advance to playoff rounds and everyone else is done for the day.. The pool size of each court will determine how long this part takes. The larger the pool the later you can expect the day to be.

Multi Day tournaments
- 2-3 days, USAV and AAU Nationals can be 4-5 days of play
- 4 team pools typically, rare occasions small as 3, large as 8 with 2 days of play,typically stay on the same court for the day of play

- Usually the best 2 out of 3 sets, standard club volleyball style play
- Every team advances to bracket play from gold to "tin foil" brackets
- Important to play and place well in the first day of pool play to maintain higher brackets
- Single match elimination during bracket/playoff play, winning team continue to play, losing team works a following match
- Entry fee required, one day or multi day, ranging in costs from $10 to $40
- Contracted vendors for venue for food. Typically costly and not athlete oriented

The volleyball F.Y.I. - If the team loses they will be expected to "work" the next match where athletes line judge, keep score, libero track, and possibly down referee the next match. Due to the size of these tournaments they come with their own nuances. Often times coolers for food nor camp chairs can be brought into the facility. If the event is not governed by food police then small snack bags of fruits, chips, peanut butter and jelly sandwiches are suggested items to have in backpacks for in between match consumption. Due to the "shared seating" for 4 teams on a court at these events camping out sideline is not advised so be sure to pack light to get up and move during the next match when your athlete's team is not on the court.

Power League

Power league volleyball tournaments are a creature all unto itself. The design of the tournament is to allow teams who might not perform as well in the first wave of play to be able to move up in to the top brackets in the second wave of play. The first wave is a typical 3-4 team pool best 2 out of 3 match play. There are two waves of play the first day which means the waves start early. There will be a 3-4 hour break and then the team will play another 3-4 team pool play by mid afternoon. If you are the mid morning wave your next wave will start 6-7 pm at night and go late. The results of the 2nd wave of play will decide what type of crossover game the team will play in the morning and then proceed onto bracket/playoff play later in the day. Once again many of these tournaments are set up in venues that have contracted vendors and the food is not necessarily athlete or cost friendly. Due to the nature of intense play it is also not a day where athletes can get a full meal in. Packing nutritious and quickly eaten snacks are important so athletes can refuel on the go. For these tournaments it is wise to start loading up the athlete with good carbohydrate rich foods and fluids days before the event so they will have fuel to burn during the event. Also a game plan of where to get a filling but not overly heavy meal after the first day of play will be key in order for athletes to get something to eat and get to bed as soon as possible. Speaking of rest it might be strongly suggested for athletes to rest between waves for the first day so be able to maintain the energy level and intensity that these types of tournaments can demand from athletes.

The volleyball F.Y.I - It is very important to talk with your athlete prior to this event about winning is not everything. Many power league tournaments are seeded from previous tournament results. The higher the seed going in the more likely the team will see the upper levels of bracket play. A lower seed is almost near impossible to find at the end of the day in the upper level brackets. It is not uncommon to see a team with a lesser win/loss ratio place ahead of a team with a better winning record. Crossover matches are a common aspect of power league tournaments. This feature is the equalizer to allow teams to move up or down from the original seeding. It is not uncommon for a team to play a 3-4 team pool of play and directly go into another match for a crossover game. Once again a reason why it is incredibly important that your athlete be properly hydrated and fueled prior to the tournament.

Qualifiers – National Championships

Qualifiers and bid tournaments are where the rubber meets the road and the team will find out how it ranks amongst other teams across the country. The purpose of qualifiers/bid tournaments to place high enough in the tournament to receive an invitation (bid) to a national championship tournament. The USAV (United States Association of Volleyball) has several qualifiers all over the country. This tournament has several levels of competition from which a team can compete in the championships. To date the Patriot level is a pay to play competition in which teams on a first come first serve basis can obtain an opportunity to play. It is important that the team should they qualify for this event are dedicated to attend it, as only the team that qualifies is able to play for the bid. If your athlete's team does not win but places high in the tournament it does not mean they will not have a chance to attend. Much like the NCAA tournament there are at large bids that are given to teams to help round out the competition. The USAV Nationals are typically the end of June to beginning of July. The AAU (Amateur Athletic Association) also has a National Championship that is traditionally mid June in Orlando,Florida. Although AAU offers opportunities to win a paid entry fee into this championship, it is a pay to play event with several levels of competition. Each are set up with either morning or afternoon wave 3-4 team pools and are from 4-5 days of play. Participation in these events can have large returns on investment as they are a hotspot for coaches of all college types that attend and a resume attractor to catch the eye of college coaches for athletes trying to set themselves apart from other athletes.

The Good, The Bad, and The Ugly

Tournaments are fabulous, exhausting, exasperating, and once in a lifetime experience with your athlete. And those are the good things. Here a few of the challenges you may come across.

- Food Nazis-Some tournaments will actually have security guards to check bags for food and water you take into the venue. Some will even turn people away to return any unacceptable items. For athletes hiding items amongst smelly kneepads or personal hygiene items will be helpful to get them past "security"
- Work Team Etiquette-Teams will have an off game but also a work game. Considering the world of teenage hierarchies they will be players that are always first to volunteer, others who will magically disappear and those who squat to do the easiest jobs at the table every game. Hopefully the coach will have a system in place to help with such challenges but if not please be sure your athlete takes turns doing the various tasks or is assertive with those who don't. It decreases dissention and

creates a better team environment. It benefits the athlete by increasing volleyball I.Q. and scouting the upcoming team in the pool.
- Second Wave Woes-For some not having to start playing at 8 a.m or 9 a.m might sound fabulous. I am here to tell you it is not unless the leisurely life is what you seek when traveling to various cities across the country. It makes it very challenging to get out to go do anything because you want your athlete to conserve energy and not be tired for tournament play, since that is the pleasure that is being paid for. But here is the big pill of it all. Should the court your athlete's team is to play on has had several 3 set matches or has had some kind of conflict to make it run behind, the 2nd wave will automatically start behind. It Is not uncommon for certain competitive tournaments to have 2nd wave match to still be playing matches at 11pm/midnight. And depending on how the team plays could very well see morning wave play the next day.

TOURNAMENT CATEGORIZATIONS

The world of volleyball is diverse and every team will have a niche that they fall into. Challenging levels of competition can be found at each level but it is important for club administrators to evaluate team makeup and ability levels and place those teams in competitions that will allow the team to put into play what they have been practicing and stretch their abilities by experiencing tougher levels of play. In a culture where everyone wants to be the best, elite, top, and many others team name adjectives it is important to remember the purpose of club volleyball and what the process is.

Club –

Club level of play can be described as developmental to advanced play. Typically these teams are local to regional teams with some travel. It is often the lowest level of competition in most tournaments.

Open –

Open level is advanced to top level college recruited play. Typically these teams are seeking the best competition and to attend post season play. They are often comprised of national travel teams or high level regional and local teams.

Mixed -

Mixed tournaments will have both club level and open level of teams playing.

Qualifiers and USAV Nationals have various levels of play which teams can qualify for. AAU also has several levels which teams can sign up for based off of the level of play the team wishes to compete in. Descriptions of these different levels can be found on the website for each competition respectively. If your athlete is expecting to attend one of these events it would be good to visit and better understand the type of experience the tournament will be.

Power Leagues –

Power leagues in our area are a selective tournament style to attract the strongest competition based on previous tournament results at that tournament and in previous competitions prior to the event. It often will include some of the most competitive clubs in a certain area or region. Other styles of power leagues are region based and have a tournament to decide who will participate in the power league for that season. Once teams are established by their performance from the initial competition they will have monthly competitions to possibly earn the opportunity to play in a championship power league tournament at the end of the season.

TOURNAMENT EXTRAS

Hotel accommodations are the big surprise for new families to club volleyball. For local and regional teams that only do one day tournaments this will not be applicable for your family. Teams that are national, travel and sometimes high level regional teams will attend tournaments that require hotel stays. Some clubs will require the team to always stay in the same hotel, blocking off rooms in advance for families to secure with their own financial information. Several highly competitive tournaments require teams to participate in a "stay to play" or "stay to save" where the tournament directors have contracted hotels in the area to block rooms for the event for a contracted price. In order for your athlete's team to compete they must block a room at those hotels. The costs of these hotels are typically in the 3 to 5 star range and often do not have free breakfast or wifi internet. Also some clubs policies require families to stay in the hotel block they have reserved. And there can be the other extreme where the club doesn't make hotel arrangements or the ones they make are poorly researched. Be sure to do the research for yourself as the details of the housing contracts and exactly where the hotel is located in comparison to the competition venue. It also helps to talk to veteran parents to learn the special nuances, great places to park and travel itineraries that are more efficient than others. Another shocking experience of the hotel experience is many venues are in developed downtown areas such as Washington D.C and Philadelphia where not only are the hotel fees high but they only have valet parking or parking that typically ranges from $30-$45 a day. If you need to drive to the venue there may be parking costs from $8 to $15 a day which can be cash only or take credit cards. Be sure to have these items handy when entering the parking garage to keep the lines moving as others will surely use the same parking areas. Some venues and cities have prepaid parking options that can be found online by googling the tournament, city, and parking. Once again this is a wise move to talk to veteran parents to find the best places or ways to find your way around the city.

Season Extras

So now the sticker shock of club fees, travel costs, and extra competition costs have put a dent in the wallet, just wait there are even more opportunities to spend hard earned cash in the club volleyball industry. Outside of entrance costs and parking fees most venues will also have vendor shopping to help you part with hard earned cash. The most popular is the tournament shirt or sweatshirt but volleyball gear such as shoes, headbands, etc can also be found, which can be convenient if your athlete happens to forget such items or breaks an ankle brace during the event.

COMBINES AND SHOWCASES

If your athlete is looking to play in college, attending at least one of these type of events is a good experience for them. The event is typically the night before the event for an entry fee from anywhere of $50 to $100. Typically these events will do some basic drills and then later have 6 players versus 6 players play against each other based off of graduation years to showcase/highlight the abilities of the athletes for college coaches to observe. Obtaining the list ahead of time will help assess the value of attending the event and for your athlete to contact potential schools they might be interested in playing for. Talking to veteran parents will let you know if the event was well organized and worth the value. The earlier your athlete can experience one of these events the better for many reasons. The first reason is to help your athlete work out the nerves in a competitive observed environment. At some point and time they will be in a tryout situation whether it is high school tryouts, USAV High Performance tryouts or college tryouts, the more times an athlete is put into those types of environments to know how it feels. The more experienced they are will result in being more prepared and able to showcase their skills in a competitive environment. The second reason is it will help your athlete evaluate their abilities to their peers in similar positions with athletes from other areas of the country. College rosters are limited and college scholarships even more so. If your athlete has high aspirations then observing the best players on the court and taking notes is the best way to figure out what it is going to be required to obtain their dreams. And lastly one of the best reasons, is the volleyball community may seem large in numbers but it is a connected community of people who follow the journey of other like minded people. Playing with other athletes that have similar desires and goals, which they may or may not have had with their team experience, is enjoyable and making connections, some of them being cross country, is icing on the cake for young athletes. Be sure to have the athlete follow up with schools after the event to get the best return on the investment and possibly even ask for feedback from college coaches. College coaches are often passionate about the game and willing to give constructive advice to players who are bold enough to ask.

USAV HIGH PERFORMANCE TRYOUTS

Many people are aware of Olympic training camps for sports such as gymnastics and winter sports. Volleyball because it is a team sport has similar opportunities to get the best athletes at various camp/competition events during the summer months. For the most elite junior athletes they will attend international competitions all expenses paid. The other programs, as one can guess, come with a pricey camp fee ranging from $500 to $1300. In order to participate in these events the athlete must attend a tryout that is held at several locations across the country, usually at large national events and qualifiers. The entry fee for a tryout is $75 to $100 depending on when you register. The early bird definitely gets the savings worm for these tryouts. Athletes tryout for an age range as determined by international regulations and can only tryout for one position per tryout. The event will test several standard skill sets and abilities in the beginning of the event. Athletes are then divided up based off of age group and position then finishing with team play based off of the evaluations made earlier in the tryout process. Once all the tryouts are complete across the country the High Performance committee evaluates the results and will assign a camp opportunity or no offer for the athlete and is posted early to mid May. More information about the National program can be found at www.teamusa.org under volleyball and High Performance. Some regional USAV programs also have High Performance team tryouts. Those teams then compete in the HP Championships in the summer for their respective region and age group. Please check with the local USAV region to find out the process and details of tryouts. For the athlete with big aspirations it is a great opportunity to be out with some of the best in the nation and they can learn much from the experience.

VIDEO/PHOTOGRAPHY

Many large events have vendors that will film or take professional pictures of your athlete. Nice extras for those wanting to capture the moment or make great gifts. It is not uncommon for photographers to come to the court to take a team picture and then create a sample for players to see during the tournament and pass amongst parents offering a volume discount. For the frugal volleyball parent, try to find another parent, sibling or someone else who can provide similar services. One parent can take raw film to distribute amongst the team to use the film editing programs of their choice.

TEAM EVENTS

Many teams will want to do activities together after the competition is done for the day. A team mom typically arranges these activities and many times it involves food. Depending on the finances, families should discuss the budget and be aware of limitations prior to attending the competition. Even if the entire family does not attend, many times parents will chaperone meals and many families are understanding when you are unable to attend. Communication with your athlete, team mom and other parents will be sure to help navigate the season.

The Good, The Bad, The Ugly

Good news is many clubs try to offer various fundraising opportunities. Companies such as Shopwithscrip.com offer easy online fundraising giving rebates for gift card purchases. Yankee Candle has online fundraising, along with local vendors such as sub and pizza sales to help athletes fund their club volleyball experience. Other club fundraising can range from selling Christmas trees, fundraising letter campaigns, referral credits, etc. If all the costs of club seem a bit overwhelming, which in all honestly it can be, please know there are ways to offset them and make club volleyball a feasible opportunity.

Return on the Investment, Recruiting

If only there was a magic formula to define the recruiting process. There is none. Too many athletes and parents have the viewpoint that attending tournaments will get their child noticed and the collegiate foot in the door. For the over the top phenom athlete who is 6 foot at age 13 years old this might be the case but for most athletes this will not be their storyline. One thing true to the industry is with the large national events, online recruiting databases, and ease of email it is a college coach's buffet. Identifying and evaluating athletes that might be a good fit for a program prior to events is easier for coaches to navigate and find the pick(s) of the club volleyball litter. If your child has big dreams and aspirations, the sooner your child should be having the college discussion of where they want to go, what they want to study and what it is they want. Also know that as your athlete matures this mindset will change so be prepared for an interesting ride. Recruiting is a marketing process and getting your child's name on the spreadsheet for coaches to know their name is one of the first steps in the recruiting process. Since there is no simple cookie cutter process here are simple steps and resources to help in the recruiting experience. Talking with the club coach, club director or even possibly the recruiting liaison at the club your athlete plays for will also help guide your family during the process. The recruiting coordinator is represented by three types active, passive, and title. The active recruiting coordinator is very active in understanding what the athlete is seeking for the future and has relations with multiple college coaches having the athlete's best interest first and foremost. The passive coordinator wants to do the best by the athlete but may not have the experience, resources, and network available to give the best assistance in the recruiting process. The title only recruiting coordinator is often a marketing role to influence parents to choose the club when shopping and comparing and does minimal to help the athlete in the recruiting process.

STEPS IN THE RECRUITING PROCESS

- Talk with your child. Define goals- short term, long term, what they want to do, college
- Sign up for recruiting site profiles and college prospective athlete forms
- Create an email address that parent and athlete can get into, work together answering emails
- Check the emails weekly, before and after tournaments
- Fill out prospective student athlete questionnaires–as many as your child thinks they

are interested in playing for or attending that school
- Contact coaches prior to, during and after tournaments. Be brief, informative, and make it personal. Use Name, Position, grad year, club, and tournament in subject heading
- STAY in contact with coaches with updates after tournaments, over the summer
- If the college has invited you to visit, and it's a school of interest, GO!
- Encourage your child to prepare, take early, and retake if necessary the PSAT, SAT, ACT. Scores mean money!
- Schools your child is interested in, go to the financial aid website, do net price calculators, and contact the school to start the discussion what will college cost for my family.
- Behave at tournaments! On the court, on the sidelines, in timeouts, and parents in the "bleachers" or camp chairs. Coaches ARE watching and they are like ninjas.
- Revisit often their goals and dreams. Where are they in their journey? Play the volleyball version

of "Would You Rather" scenarios to help the athlete think ahead and how they might feel with the potential different options they could face.
- Showcases and combines are beneficial but not necessary. Contact coaches before for maximum potential.
- Take video of your child playing or make arrangements with someone who is filming
- Edit and/or upload film. Be sure to mute the sound. No Eye of the Tiger music is necessary
- Consider making a simple website that has footage links and press links of your child's play
- Encourage your child to do the website themselves and BLOG about their experience in a positive way. Remember it's about marketing the best you!
- D1 schools shop early. D2 schools shop early junior year to early senior year, D3 will prospect junior year but a majority of talks start the senior year.
- Remember it's a process more like a marathon with no map, not a sprint. There are lots of turns and uphills. Possibly some downhills but do not be

discouraged. Keep searching for the opportunities that best fit your child's goals academically and is the best fit for them athletically.
- Carpe Diem – Seize the day. Every time your child is on the court there is an opportunity possibly waiting for your child. Club is also an investment towards their future, get the best value out of your money. Be sure to do the homework, encourage your child to love the game, remind them to make every ball count in practice and at tournaments, and dream big.
- Questions often asked by college coaches and should ask the athlete in the college search
    - What are you looking for in your college experience? ie. Size, location, student body of school, social aspects, academic goals, athletic goals
    - What do you like about ___school? Or how did you find that school?
    - What do you like to do in or away from volleyball?

Conclusion

Club volleyball has many benefits for the athlete. It gives opportunities to grow and develop physically, mentally and emotionally in the sport. Learning to adapt and interact with a variety of personalities and circumstances that all too often mimic the adult "real" world. For families it provides the experience of self advocacy, independence, and family bonding during club season that is rich in memories and growth opportunities. The good, the bad, and the ugly are also a part of the club volleyball experience in which seeking out information, advice from seasoned participants, and keeping focus on the goals set out by athletes and families will help during those times.

Best of play to the volleyball athlete and family.

About the Author

Hello and thank you for taking the time to read this book. We have been through many adventures and challenges throughout our years so far and I am sure we are not done. My goal in writing this was to help give a basic foundation of information to help guide families coming in to the sport some direction and understanding. Managed expectations always seem to have better results for everyone involved and most of all for families who have so much invested time, emotionally, and definitely financially. Also please know that this book is mostly based off of experiences and club volleyball in the east coast region in which I live. Other areas may be structured differently so it is important to learn as much as possible when choosing to whether to participate in club volleyball.

When my first child decided to play club volleyball she was a sophomore and we were extremely limited in our knowledge about the sport. She did exceptionally well for her first year, almost making a national team and qualifying for the USAV High Performance A2 program, and making the regional team to participate in the High Performance Championships. I spent most of the season talking with experienced parents, coaches, and reading as much as I possibly could. I had a lot of sticker shock challenges being a family of 9 with 1.75 incomes. We had many peanut butter and jelly moments but we managed. Also at the same time my oldest daughter decided to play club volleyball. Her experience was less than desired to say the least but she did manage to grow in the sport and play well in a Division 3 college. Since then we have funded and balanced up to 3 athletes playing at 2 different clubs at one time, my one daughter playing for one of the most elite clubs in the area driving 2 hours one way/4 hours round trip 3 times a week and traveling legitimately all over the country, and having been a part of 6 clubs total in our area, and not all by first choice but due to team collapses 3 different times.

We have had 34 college visits to date with one athlete still to go. My daughter who started this club volleyball adventure had to decide between a full ride scholarship her freshman year to a Division 1 school, a favorite Division 2 school with scholarship monies available her sophomore year, and a top five Division 3 school with a pretty good academic scholarship. My college tip advice, college visits are everything for athletes to help in their decisions and preferably start EARLY! The Division 1 school had a Penn State alum which my daughter fangirled over and had they offered her monies during her visit she would not have fallen in love the very next day at the Division 3 school where she attends to date. The scholarship offer came when their first choice was unable to get accepted to the school academically and they offered my daughter the scholarship just days before May 1st deadline. It was hard for her to turn down her hoped goal of a college scholarship but her heart was already set. My oldest daughter was an easy sell as she received a $52,000 financial aid package for a $54,000 school and it was a place she could play volleyball. Signed, sealed and delivered. At the moment my third daughter is the midst of making her decision and I truly hope it will not take till May like her sisters. My last athlete will probably be the most adventurous. Her list of potential schools range from a few Division 1 schools to several Division 2 schools to multiple Division 3 schools, many of them attending the NCAA Championship tournaments in past years which will translate to many college visits during an already crammed packed club season.

As a parent I have gone from newbie parent who probably overreacted at times to a more balanced less reactive parent to the situations that present themselves during club season. Thank you to the club directors who tolerated me during the years. I am not quite convinced that the return on investment in relation to college scholarship payoff has been as beneficial as I had initially hoped for. So I would advise if you are only having your child play club volleyball for a college scholarship, you may want to reevaluate that being the only goal. When attending club tournaments take a look around and count the amount of girls in your child's age group and then multiply that by at least 30 other tournaments possibly going on that weekend. Coaches have pick the of the litter opportunities at these events and limited scholarships to offer. The return on investment that I can say has overflowed my expectations is the life experiences/growth and memories I have shared with my athletes and family as a result of club volleyball. As a parent I have been presented with opportunities to help them be critical thinkers, overcome adversity, and celebrate their success. We have been all over the country Minnesota, Las Vegas, Missouri, Chicago, Indianapolis, North Carolina, Virginia, Washington D.C and Florida to name some of the bigger venues. Without club volleyball I can probably say we would have never traveled to such places.

Many times throughout this journey I have stepped back and thought "When did I become that parent?" You know the ones that prior to club sports that people think are crazy to spend so much money and time for their child to play a sport. Although I do find it odd that people don't say that about teeball and little league football. Maybe that is because they are smaller and the cost isn't as much. The sport of women's volleyball is growing by leaps and bounds. If your child is looking to play in college then club volleyball is at this point probably essential. And even though in the eyes of other parents I might seem crazy to have done so, club volleyball for my athletes has made their world better and helped them achieve their desires to play better, stronger and the game they love. It has been completely worth every minute and every dollar.

Best of play and journey to you and yours.

~~~COMING SOON ~~~
Recruiting Buddy – Recruiting Workbook
Basics to help get the process started
         and stay organized

APPENDIX
RECRUITING RESOURCES
Recruting websites

NCSA – http://www.ncsasports.org/   Has a free sign up, a pay sign up, very pricey

University athlete - https://universityathlete.com/ Important to have a club affiliation to sign up. Many college coaches use this resource to identify athletes at events that they may not have had previous contact with.

Be Recruited - https://new.berecruited.com/

Athlete Vision - http://athletevisionsports.com/   Used by several combines, tournaments and records video of your child.

Sports Recruits- http://sportsrecruits.com offers a free guide about recruiting. (NOT FREE)

CaptainU - http://learn.captainu.com/   (less known)

SportForce- http://www.sportsforceonline.com/ (less known)

Rich Kern recruiting registry - http://www.recruitingregistry.com/

National Athletes-http://www.nationalathletes.com/

National Scouting Report - http://www.nsr-inc.com/

Informational Newsletters/Websites
Informed Athlete- http://informedathlete.com/ free email-for up to date information about recruiting
College Essentials
College Data. Com -College Match search engine http://www.collegedata.com/
National Clearinghouse (D1 and D2 interested) http://web1.ncaa.org/ECWR2/NCAA_EMS/NCAA.jsp or just google National Clearinghouse it might be easier

NAIA Eligibility Clearinghouse http://www.playnaia.org/

StartClass – http://colleges.startclass.com - search engine to compare colleges by:
Key facts, Rankings, Admissions, Costs and Expenses, Financial Aid, Academics
Student Body, Sports, Post-Graduation, Notable, Alumni, College, Crime, College Scorecard

PLAYER QUESTIONNAIRE

Top 3 dream schools   Top 3 Good schools   Top 3 safe schools
1.
2.
3.

What do I want to be when I grow up?

What is your dream job?

Circle the answer that best fits you
A competitive program is
Not very important   Either way is ok
The best part of the game

Playing time versus the win column
Not very important   Either way is ok
Wanna be on the court

Campus size is
Not very important   Doesn't matter
Very important to my decision

<u>Prospective   Student   Athlete – Recruiting Questionnaire form information</u>

Name   **Birthdate**
Grad year
Address
Mobile Number

Other contact person's info (this is usually the parent who is most involved in helping you)

Mom occupation, phone, cell, email, alma mater

Dad occupation, phone,cell, email, alma mater

Siblings,ages

Major interest   (may want to list a couple)

High school name, address, phone number

High school Counselor's name, phone number, email, fax number

High school coach name, phone number, email

Club coach name, phone number, email , club website

Your jersey number/color
Standing reach
Approach Reach
Block Jump
Primary position
Dominant Hand
Height   Weight
Letters Won in this sport
Individual Honors

Additional sports
SAT Scores   Total   Math   Reading
   Writing   Date Taken   Retake?
ACT Scores Total
   Date Taken   Retake?
GPA   Rank(X out of X)
Academic Honors

Do you have a recruiting website?
      Send web address
Additional Coach references name, email, phone

Are you registered with NCAA Eligibility center, If yes then what is your ID#

Have you applied to this school, date applied

Will you be asking for financial aid? Have you filled out the FASFA?

What other colleges are you looking at?
                              (usually top 3-5)

Career Statistics(include personal best times):
All-Conference honors in career (first team as a junior, etc.)
Other Athletic Honors in Career (all-state, all-area, etc.
Team Highlights in career *Have a copy of your transcript in a word document to upload

GLOSSARY OF TERMS

6 on 6 drills – Volleyball activity where teams of 6 on each side play/scrimmage each other to incorporate skills learned in practice to game like situations.

AAU – Amateur Athletic Union is an organization overseeing many amateur sports through competitions, including nationals.

Camp – A planned volleyball event that can be a single day to several days. Typically a larger fee than a clinic and often includes meals, athlete breaks, and supervised activities.

Cap - To limit game play time some tournaments will define a cap where the 2 point rule would be nullified. If the game cap is 28, the first team to 28 points regardless of point spread will win.

Clinic- A volleyball event that is like a practice for athletes wanting to improve skills or learn new aspects of the game. Typically done for a fee and can be done by athletes and coaches.

Combine – A volleyball event designed to evaluate and assess certain volleyball skills often for the viewing of college coaches.

Court position – Spots on the court are often given numbers

4	3	2
5	6	1

to indicate where an athlete is playing on the court.

Club or Travel Volleyball – Teams that play volleyball for a fee, typically regulated by a governing body. Teams are formed to play in competitions in the region or nation.

Crossover game – A component of a volleyball tournament to mix up the competition and give opportunities for teams to be able to play in higher playoff levels. It is also used to equalize pools/games played that may not have had as many teams in their pool due to an uneven team registration.

Defensive Specialist – A volleyball position where the player plays mostly in the back row attempting to pass the balls from the opposing team during serves or game play.

Director – Typically the top level administrator in a club volleyball organization.

JVA – Junior Volleyball Association is an trade association/organization that helps develop standards for club volleyball and coordinates competitions.

Libero – A volleyball position where the player wears a different colored jersey and is able to move in and out of the game for various athletes in the back row. This athlete is not required to participate in substitution requirements and allows for fewer stoppages during a game.

Libero tracking – A task during a volleyball match, performed by the opposing team currently not playing on the court, to keep track of the libero coming in and out of the court.

Line judge – A person who stands at the corners of a volleyball court and watches for serving infractions, whether a ball falls inside the game of play, and if players touch a ball prior to exiting the court. Many tournaments use opponent team members that are currently not playing a match on the court.

Match - The terminology used for volleyball game comprised typically of two sets to 25 and one set to 15 if both teams win a set.

Match/set point – The recognition of the point by the referee on the floor (down referee) to the up ref (the referee on the stand at the net) that the point being played could end the set/match.

Middle, middle hitter, middle blocker – The volleyball position played in the front row in the middle. A fast paced offensive position which requires the opposing player to also be fast at deterring (blocking) the play.

Open gym – A volleyball event where athletes can play to experience the volleyball atmosphere and become acquainted with staff and coaches. Typically a free event with minimal structure or skills instruction.

Pin hitter, outside, right side, opposite – The volleyball position played in the front row on either the right or left hand side. The purpose of this player is to get into position to be able to hit the ball so that the opposing team cannot return the ball

Position – The title of job descriptions in a volleyball game. Setter, middle, opposite/right side, outside, pin hitter (both outside or right side position), middle(middle blocker, middle hitter) defensive specialist, and libero are typically the positions offered. Utility players are players that can play a variety of roles on the court. Serving specialist is a player who would only participate in serving for a play and playing for that point rotation till the serve is lost by the team.

Positional/Skills practice – A practice that is geared specifically to increasing the knowledge regarding a specific volleyball position and/or skill that can include multiple age groups and club branches.

Qualifier/bid tournament – A tournament type that if participated in and place high enough will qualify/allow a team to play in a national tournament at the end of the club season. USAV levels of bids are; Open, National, USA, American, and Patriot. AAU National levels are Open, Premier, Club, Aspire, and Classic.

Rotation – The volleyball game is played where when each team gets the opportunity to serve the players move in location clockwise to a different location/spot on the court thus called a rotation.

Set – The parts of a volleyball match that is typically played to 25 or 15 points. In club volleyball typically 3 sets make a match.

Setter – The volleyball position, like the quarterback in football, that strategizes the game play and runs the offense for the team.

Showcase – A volleyball event designed to allow athletes to perform for the purpose of being watched by college coaches.

Single elimination – One set/match of pre-determined points. Often used in smaller tournaments during quarterfinal and semi final matches to decrease time length of the tournament.

"Stay to play" or "Stay to save" - These tournament types are competitions that require teams to stay in pre-contracted hotels in order to compete. Some competitions have mile limitations as to what is considered "out of town" and some contracts only require a percentage of rooms be booked to fulfill the contract.

Strength and conditioning - Exercise regimens designed for volleyball athletes to develop muscle strength and endurance needed to play at higher intensity of play.

Team pools - The structure of volleyball tournaments to divide teams into groups that will be played on one court consecutively till all opponents have played one another.

Travel Cost – The cost outside of club fees/dues for hotels (often in city areas), hotel parking, transportation, airfare, and food costs/dining out.

Tryout – A planned volleyball event where volleyball club staff will evaluate athletes for the potential of being asked to play on a club team. Typically done for a fee, overseen and planned by the local governing volleyball organization. Tryouts can vary per club and region.

USAV (USA Volleyball) – the nonprofit organization recognized internationally as the governing body of volleyball for the United States.

Volleyball IQ – The basic understanding of the workings of the game of volleyball. Much like Algebra there are many levels of knowledge as to how the game works. As the level of athleticism and understanding of the game increases so does the need for the volleyball I.Q. to increase.

Win/loss differentials - Smaller tournaments use the amount of points a team wins by and loses by to rank teams for the playoff rounds. A team that wins by 10 one set and loses by 8 in another set has a win/loss differential of plus 2 points (+2)

For more information, questions, or to request the Volley Blogging Mom to come to speak, contact her at volleybloggingmom@gmail.com

Follow her on these sites:

Facebook:
www.facebook.com/volleybloggingmom

Twitter:
www.twitter.com/VballmomSelene

Instagram:
www.instagram.com/volleybloggingmom

Website:
www.volleybloggingmom.com

Printed in Great Britain
by Amazon

72635566R00045